Recipe for Laughter:
Book of Cooking Cartoons

Featuring Cartoons From
Air Mail
Esquire
The New Yorker
and more!

Front Cover illustration: Amy Hwang
Back Cover illustration: Roz Chast
Introduction: Bob Mankoff
Design: Darren Kornblut
Layout: Adam Kornblut

Dedicated to Bonnie who loves to cook,
Jennifer & Bea

Cartoon Collections, LLC
10 Grand Central, 29th Floor
New York, NY 10017

For cartoon licensing information visit www.cartoonstock.com

First edition published 2024
ISBN: 978-1-963079-01-2
Item # 46493

Introduction

Imagine you're slicing an onion, but instead of tears, you're shedding laughs. That's what we're aiming for in this culinary cartoon collection. In the grand tradition of humor that finds its way into every crevice of life, we've turned our pens and wits towards the kitchen, a place as ripe with comedy as it is with tomatoes.

Each page serves up a fresh course of laughter, seasoned with a pinch of sarcasm and a dollop of absurdity, perfectly paired with a side of insightful commentary on our food-obsessed culture. Whether you're a Michelin-starred chef or someone who considers cereal a viable dinner option, there's something in here to tickle your taste buds and your funny bone.

Remember, the heart of comedy is timing - too much and you overcook the joke, too little and it falls flat. In these pages, you'll find the comedic timing has been finely honed to perfection, much like the blade of a well-kept chef's knife. So, tie on your apron, preheat your sense of humor, and prepare to feast on a banquet of cartoons that celebrate the chaos, joy, and, above all, the fun of cooking. Bon appétit!

"If we double the temperature, it'll be finished in half the time."

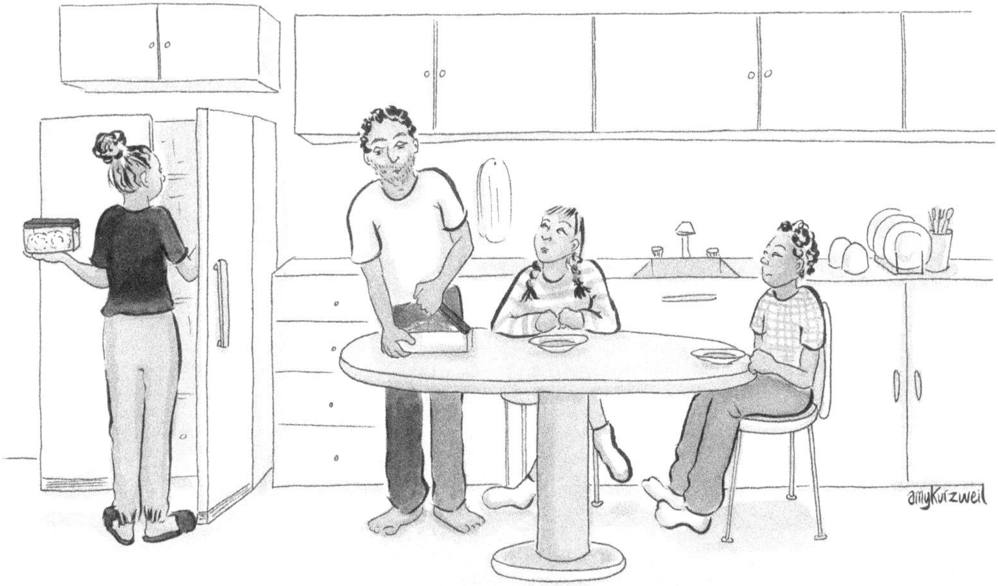
amyKurzweil

FRIDGE-TO-TABLE

"I enjoy root vegetables as much as anyone, but enough is enough."

"But do your mittens smell like chocolate chip cookies?"

RECIPES FROM HILLARY'S KITCHEN

HILLARY'S SALAD

Destroy a head of lettuce with your bare hands and toss with a red pepper that has been hacked to pieces. Drown in a light vinaigrette.

CHELSEA'S FAVORITE COOKIES

Pulverize flour, sugar, butter, eggs, and baking soda. Drop resentfully by teaspoonfuls on cookie sheet and incinerate.

There! Happy now?

CHICKEN À LA RODHAM

Whack a roaster into submission with a blunt object. Then hurl insults at it until tender. "Serves" six.

"Oh, no—Karen baked a cake so dense that not even light can escape."

"Oh, knock it off! It's only cream of asparagus."

"I make big batches and freeze it."

"Looks like it's time to make the banana bread."

"*I love it. Who did it?*"

"By the time we got there, all we wanted to do was raid their kitchen."

"How am I supposed to cook? The internet is down."

"...brisket ...recipe. Hide it."

"I vary her diet with a wide variety of pasta shapes."

"You're lost. This is Mom's apple pie."

"*Are you as excited as I am?*"

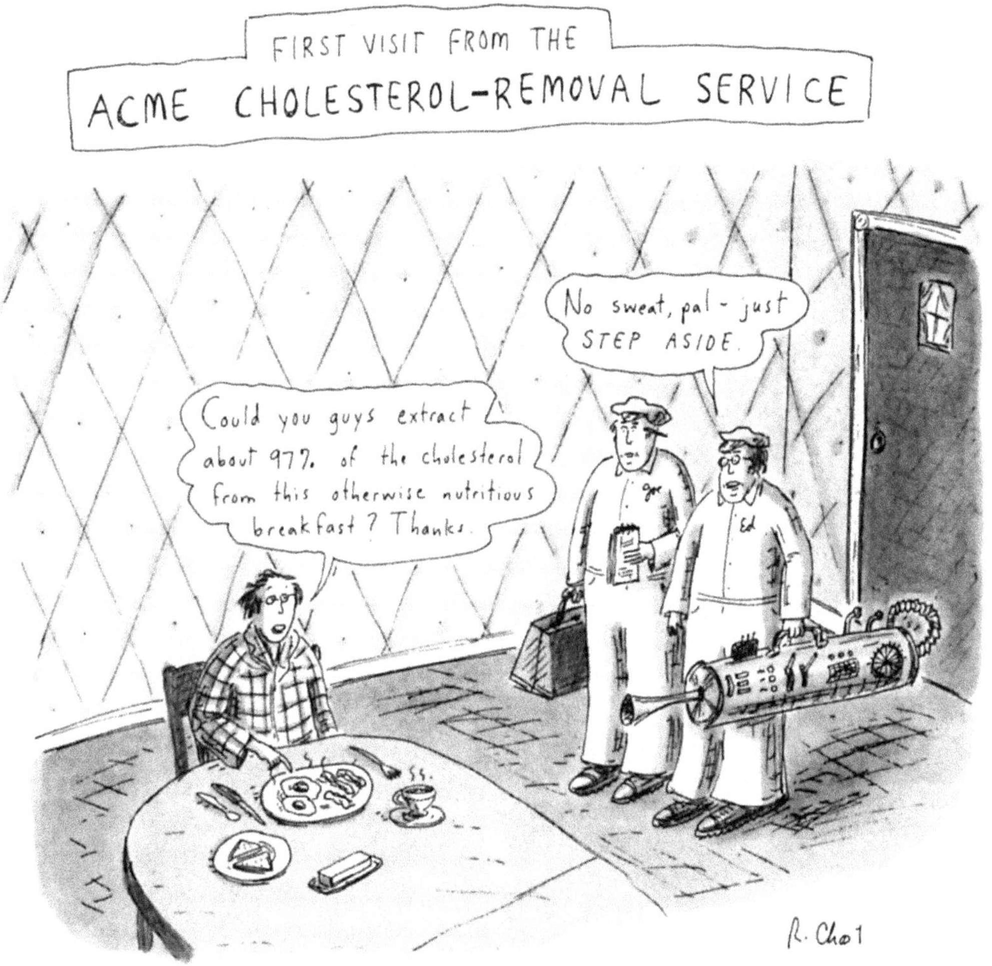
FIRST VISIT FROM THE
ACME CHOLESTEROL-REMOVAL SERVICE
Could you guys extract about 97% of the cholesterol from this otherwise nutritious breakfast? Thanks.
No sweat, pal - just STEP ASIDE.
R. Chast

JUNK DRAWER

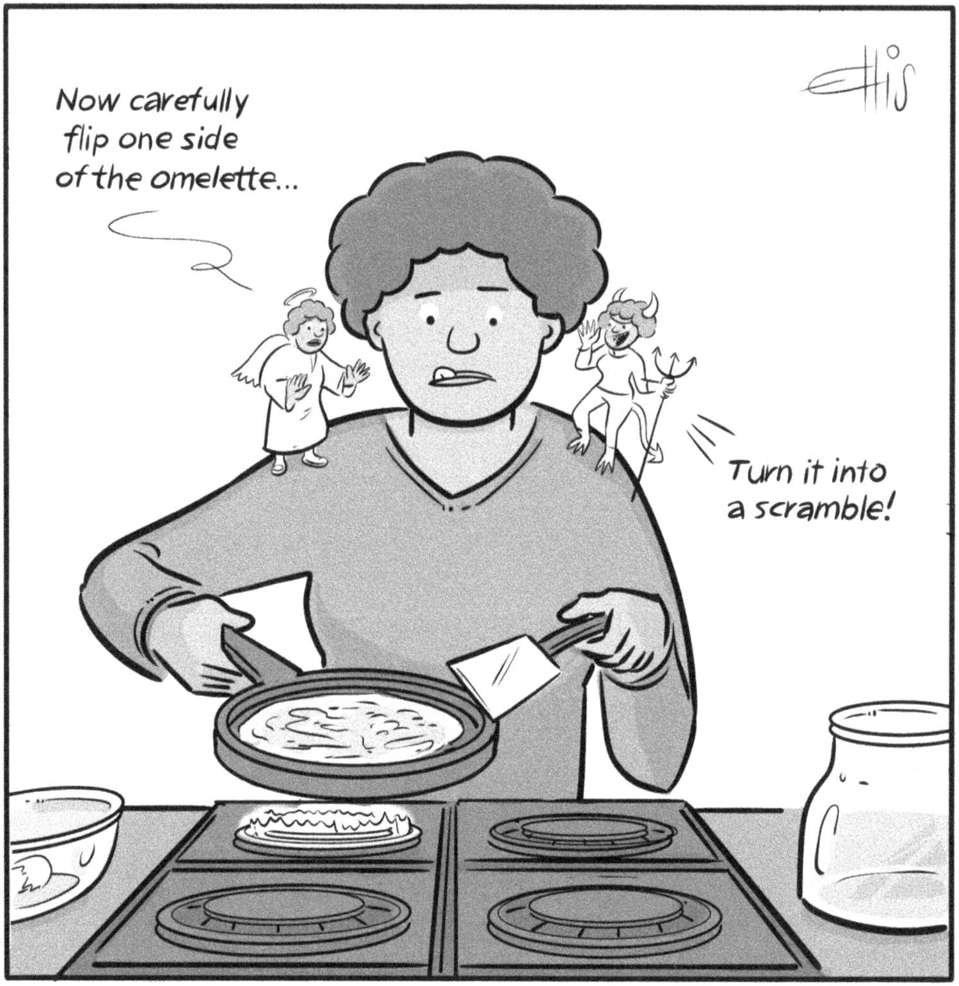
Now carefully flip one side of the omelette...
Turn it into a scramble!

"O.K. Fair enough. That's a great price for mayonnaise."

"Do you want brownies or cookies
or banana bread or apple pie or peanut brittle
or chocolate muffins or carrot cake?"

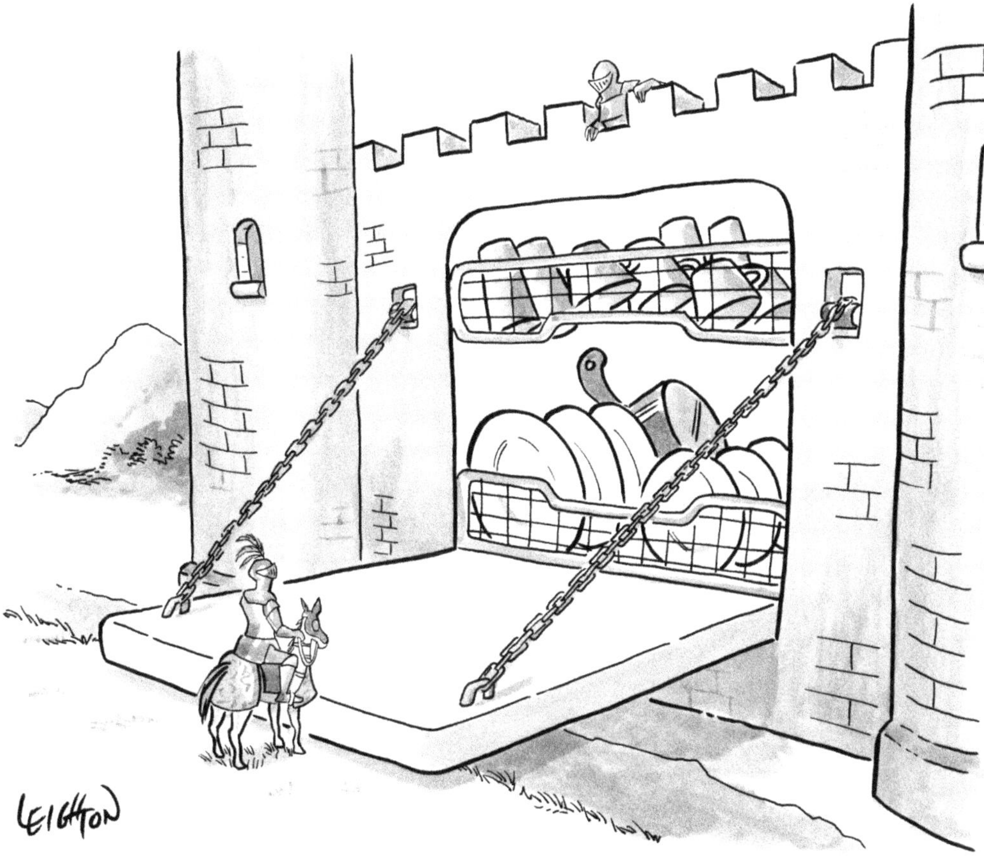
LEIGHTON

GOOD FOR YOU
BUT
TASTE LOUSY

BAD FOR YOU
BUT
TO DIE FOR

J. di Chiarro

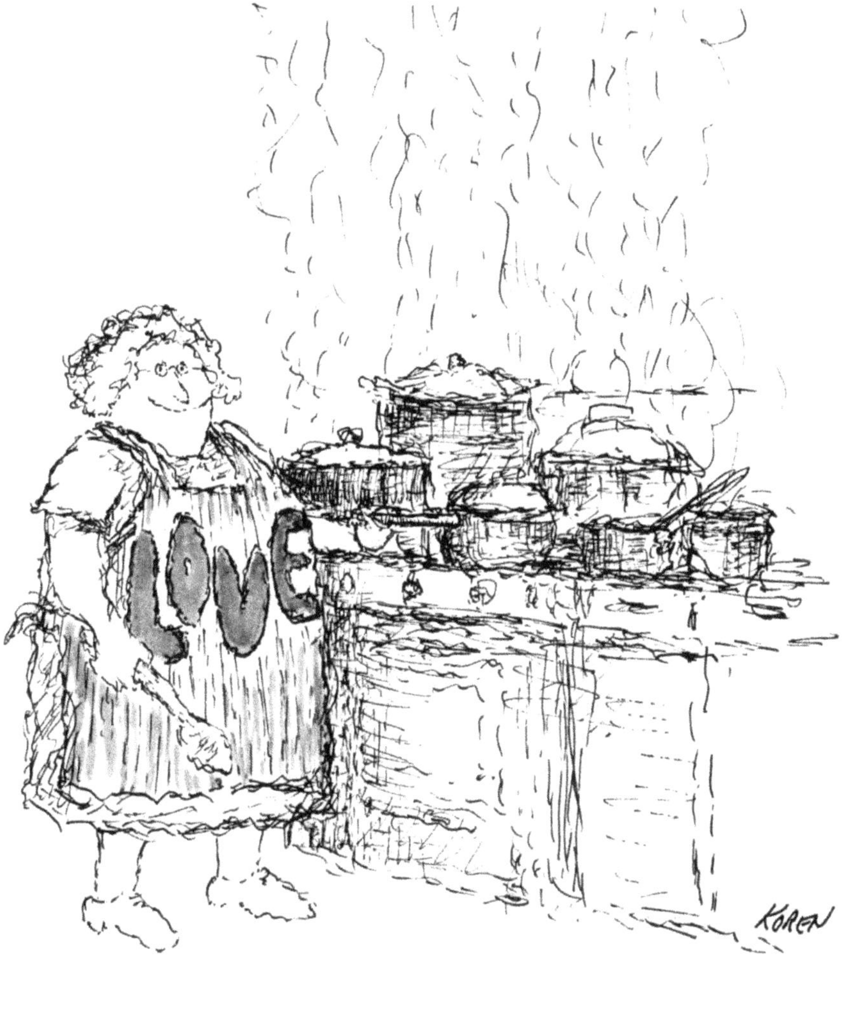
LOVE
KOREN

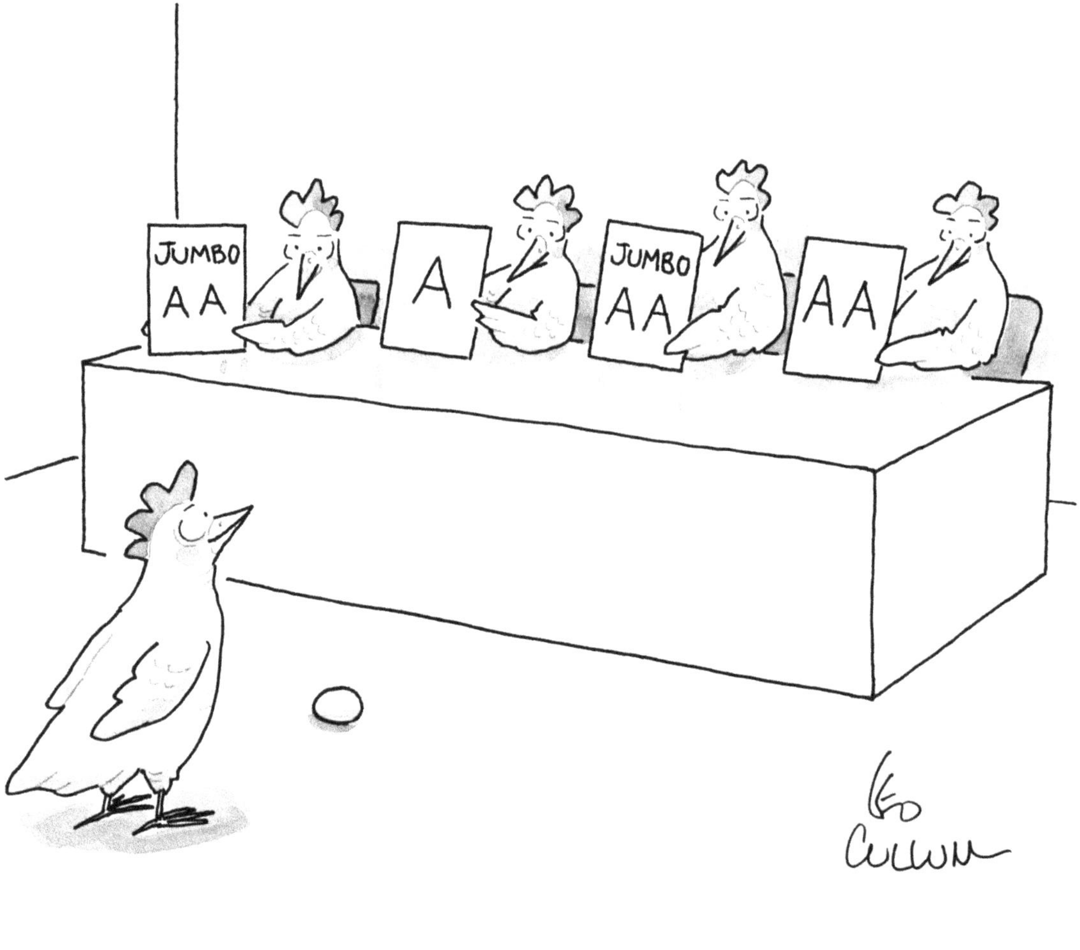
JUMBO
AA
A
JUMBO
AA
AA
Leo Cullum

WELCOME TO
THE MUSEUM OF ONE'S KITCHEN

The Refrigerator Door Gallery

Don't try to absorb it all in one visit.

The Cabinet of Too Many Teas

Not even the curator knows why there are so many.

The Shelf of Antiquity

Products from before the dawn of time.

The Mark and Janine Bostwick Impulse Buy Collection

On exhibit this week.

26

"*I cooked us a lovely dinner for two—you could at least do the dishes!*"

"Don't be intimidated. He doesn't even have a balcony."

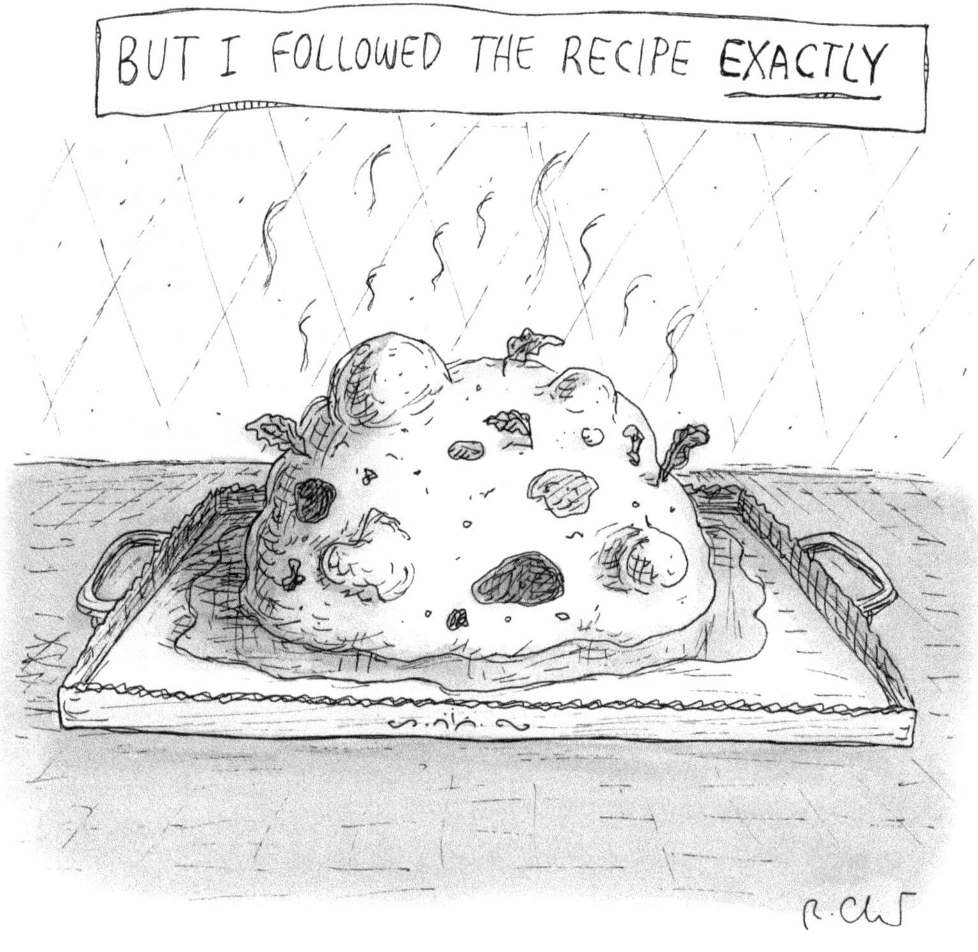
BUT I FOLLOWED THE RECIPE EXACTLY

THE IRON CHEF AT HOME

YUCK! What smells so DISGUSTING?

Why can't we just order a pizza, like everyone else?

Whatever it is you're making, it sure is using a lot of pots and pans.

LIVING ALONE

IT'S JUST PLAIN FUN!

THE 60-HOUR GOURMET

RECIPES FOR PEOPLE WHO HAVE TIME TO SPARE, AND THEN SOME

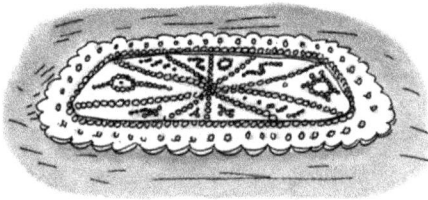

Painstakin' Peas

Before cooking, peel six hundred peas. Boil. Then arrange in a festive manner on a serving platter.

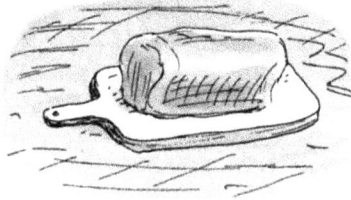

Never-Ending Bread

Mix bread dough as usual. Let rise until double. Punch down. Let rise again. Punch down. Let rise. Punch down. Let rise. Punch down. Rise. Punch. Rise, punch, rise, punch, rise. Bake and serve.

Slow 'n' Steady Chicken

Wash chicken in a lukewarm bubble bath for ± one hour. Then rinse for thirty minutes. Stuff with Difficult Stuffing*, using a doll spoon, and truss with an itsy-bitsy needle and the teensy-weensiest stitch you can. Cook at 125°F. for 32 hours. Just prior to serving, carve into the shape of a rose.

* see page 883

Handmade Carrot Juice

Begin by mincing raw carrots with a butter knife. Then keep going until the whole thing reaches a liquid consistency.

R. Chr

FORMERLY BAD.
NOW GOOD FOR YOU.

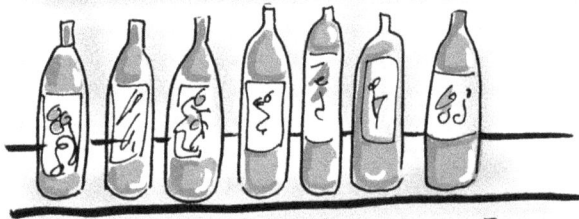

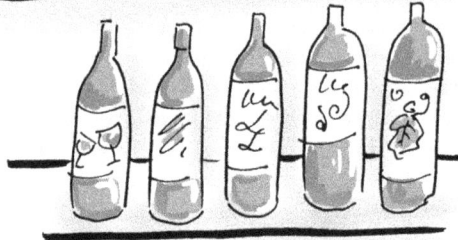

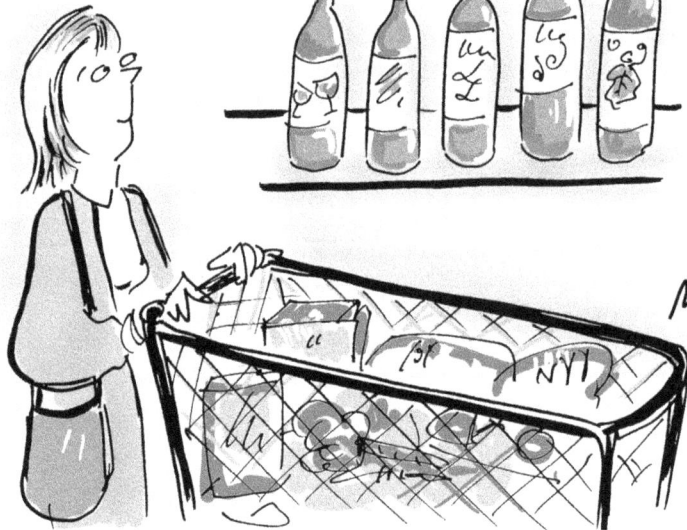

THE NERVOUS GOURMET

This week: **LOW-RISK CHICKEN**

1. Get or pay someone to light the oven for you.
2. Place chicken in oven using six-foot tongs.
3. Bake it for 1-1½ hours while you are close enough to make sure that the heat from the oven isn't setting anything on fire, but far enough away so that if, by any chance, the oven should explode, you will escape with only minor injuries.
4. Make arrangements to have someone remove chicken from oven while you stand at the opposite end of the kitchen.
5. Put on oven mitt and turn off oven.

YOUR FRIEND

Next week: **TOAST WITHOUT ANXIETY**

R. Chost

"Ideally, you want the dough to rise to about
thirty-five thousand feet."

"Set oven to five hundred degrees. While preheating, get stepladder and turn off smoke alarm. Then season brisket, chop herb medley, and turn of smoke alarm again. Resume chopping herb medley, peel potatoes, slip off stepladder while agrily trying to remove the battery from the smoke alarm ..."

"Keep in mind, this dish is best served in a restaurant cooked by anyone other than you."

"Should we try that new place in the corner?"

"No, I don't want to play chess. I just want you to reheat the lasagna."

HELP YOURSELF
Care for one?
They're really good.
Why don't you take some home?
No pressure.
R. Chast

"Everything I needed to know I learned from my mother – but I usually follow up with a YouTube video for verification purposes."

WHEEL OF DINNER

Don't be so hard on yourself. No one in this city cooks.

Except Brad. Brad and all of his food pictures on Instagram.

Cereal.

The two chicken nuggets all the way at the back of the freezer.

Does hummus go bad?

Takeout tonight and then I swear I'll grocery shop tomorrow.

dko

"You're the first person I've met who didn't become a pastry chef after suffering a nervous breakdown in a corporate job."

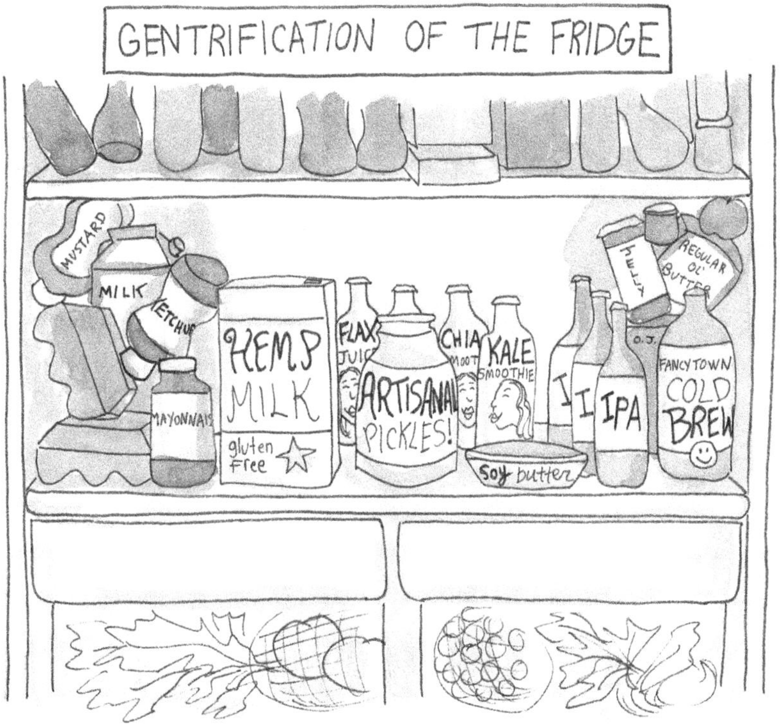
GENTRIFICATION OF THE FRIDGE
MUSTARD
MILK
KETCHUP
MAYONNAIS
HEMP MILK
gluten free
FLAX
ARTISANAL PICKLES!
CHIA
KALE SMOOTHIE
soy butter
IPA
JELLY
REGULAR OL' BUTTER
O.J.
FANCYTOWN COLD BREW

amy kurzweil

"Hold on—I think you got my toast."

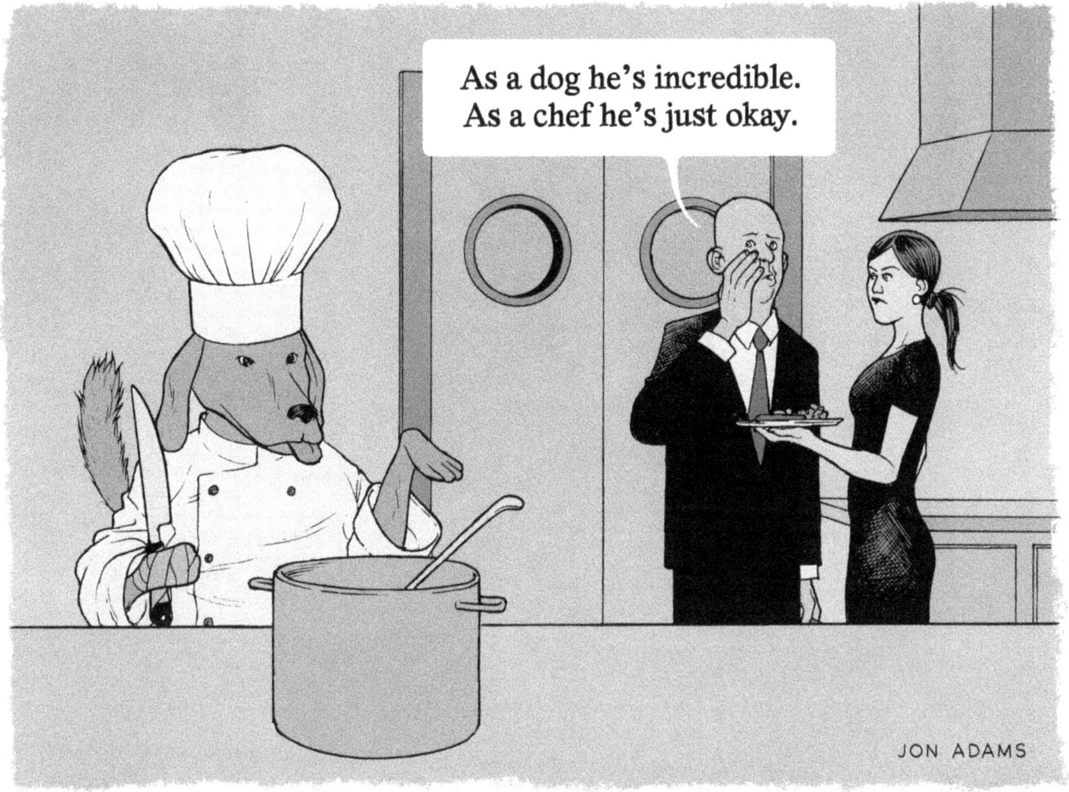
As a dog he's incredible. As a chef he's just okay.
JON ADAMS

"I freeze all my leftovers until I feel less
guilty about throwing them away."

"When you have a moment would
you mind browning the meringue?"

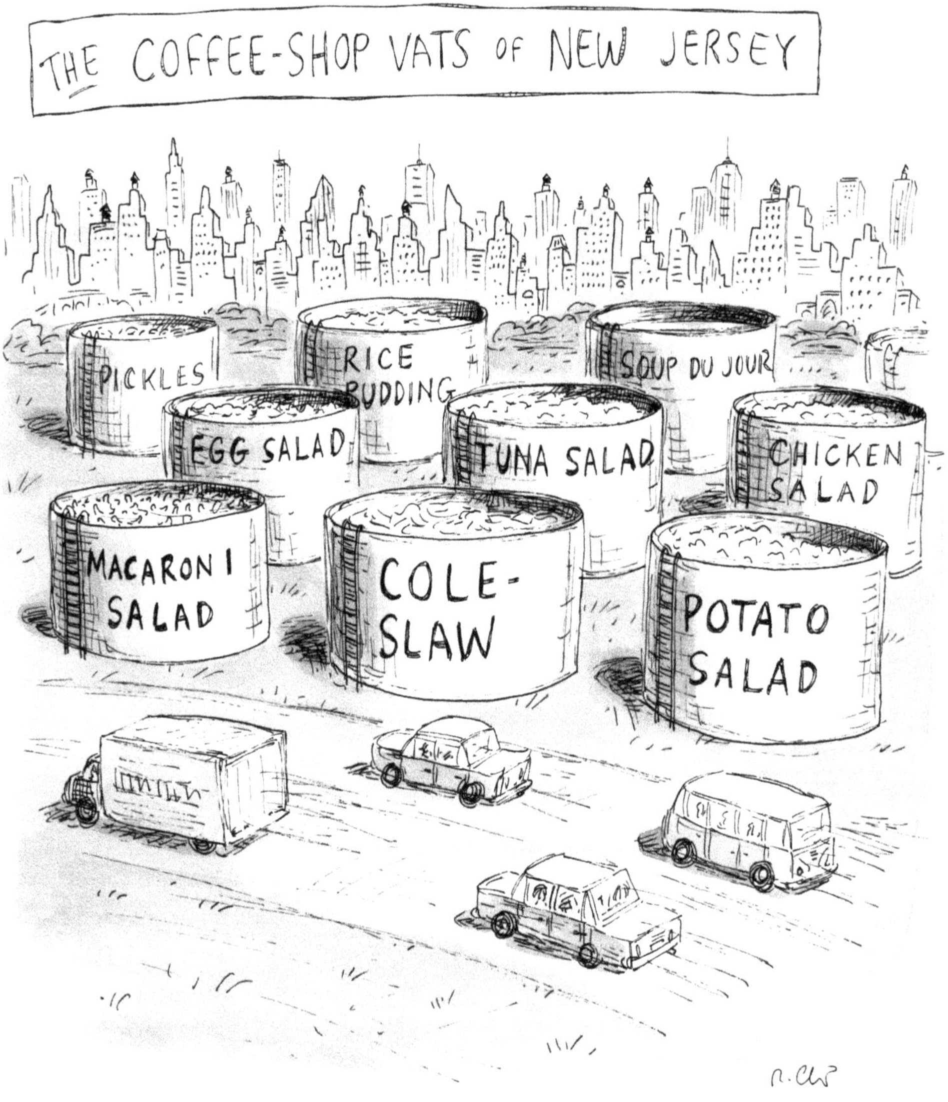
THE COFFEE-SHOP VATS OF NEW JERSEY
PICKLES
RICE PUDDING
SOUP DU JOUR
EGG SALAD
TUNA SALAD
CHICKEN SALAD
MACARONI SALAD
COLE-SLAW
POTATO SALAD

"Don't worry. This year I have a new recipe."

"So this where the magic happens."

"Then bake at 375 for forty-five minutes."

"We've come to spoil the broth."

"Yes, you could have cooked it, but you didn't."

"The problem is that your trap is one big macaroni."

"*It's meatloaf. We didn't make our Kickstarter goal for steak.*"

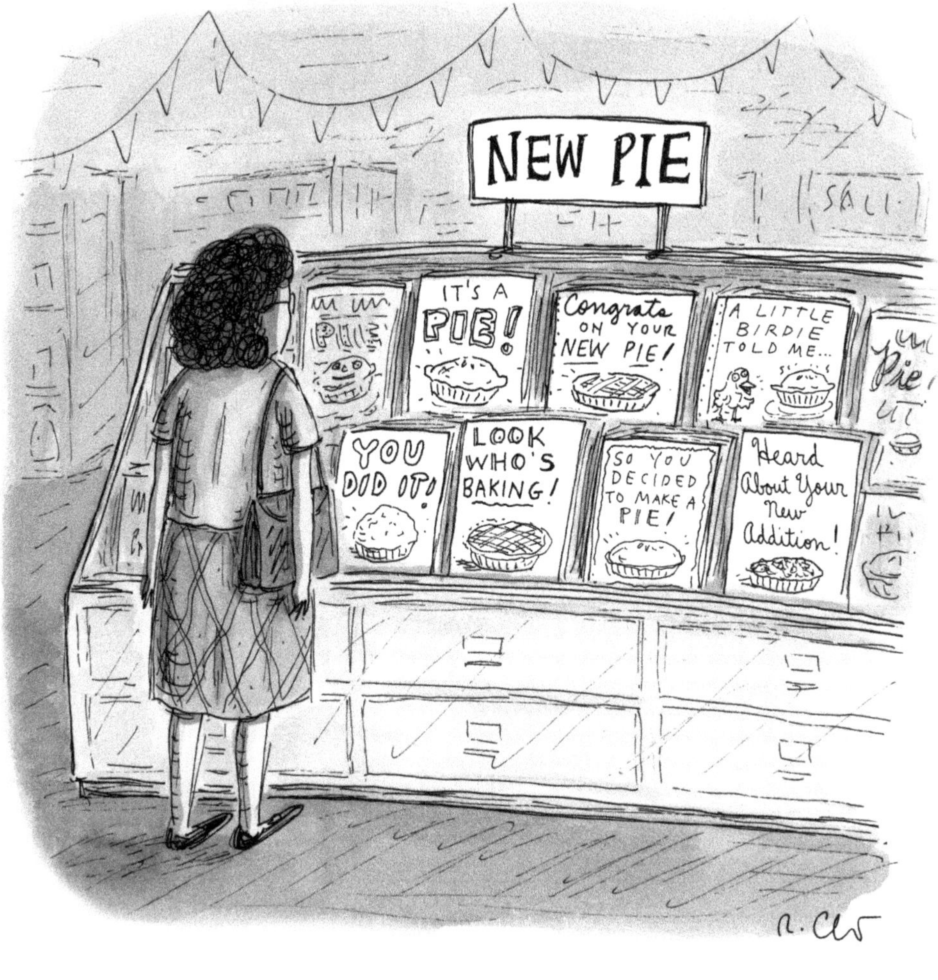
NEW PIE
IT'S A PIE!
Congrats ON YOUR NEW PIE!
A LITTLE BIRDIE TOLD ME...
YOU DID IT!
LOOK WHO'S BAKING!
SO YOU DECIDED TO MAKE A PIE!
Heard About Your New Addition!

"Kids! No watching Bobby Flay before Mommy cooks dinner!"

"Bob sacrifices the first burger
to the barbecue gods."

"Yeah, but 20,000 people liked mine."

"They said that creating an alphabet soup was a bad idea, but I will make them eat their words."

"You missed the garlic. The place went nuts when he added the garlic."

"Well, there's your problem right there—you need to saute the onions in white wine before adding the ginger."

TOO MANY LAWYERS SPOIL THE BROTH

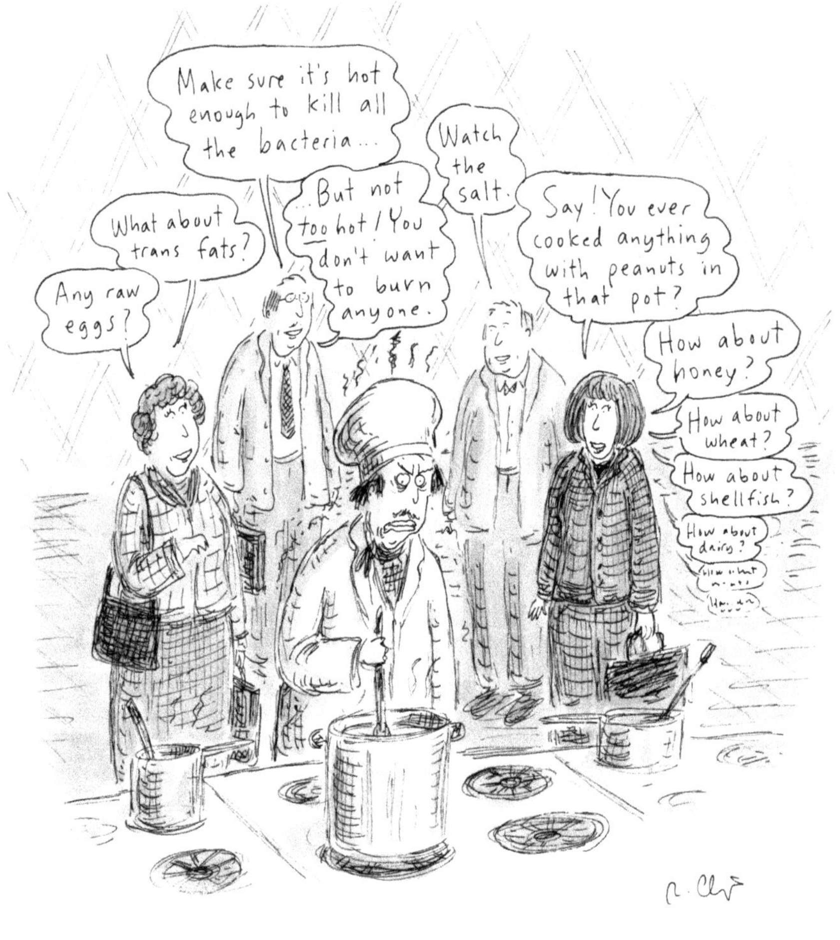

Any raw eggs?
What about trans fats?
Make sure it's hot enough to kill all the bacteria...
...But not too hot! You don't want to burn anyone.
Watch the salt.
Say! You ever cooked anything with peanuts in that pot?
How about honey?
How about wheat?
How about shellfish?
How about dairy?

"The wings are addictive."

"I don't bake, I don't cook, but I make one kick-ass vinaigrette."

"Well, that guy has the cool hat, but the other guy is actually cooking."

"Well, the crazy bastards went ahead and did it...
they wrapped it in bacon."

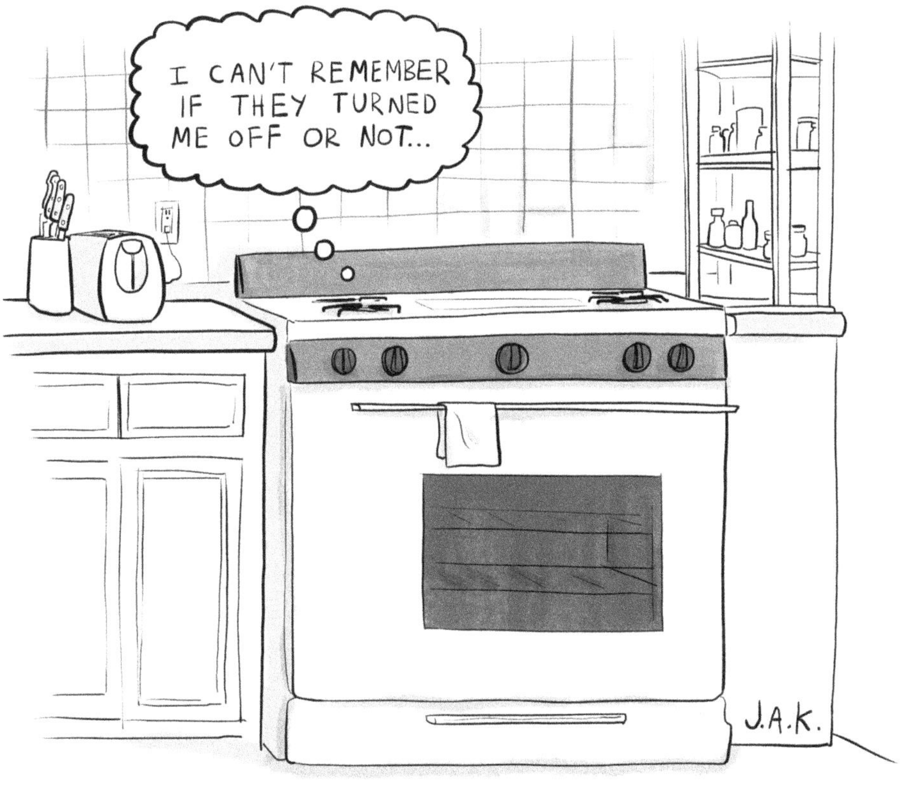
I CAN'T REMEMBER IF THEY TURNED ME OFF OR NOT...
J.A.K.

"I stuffed it with things found around the house."

"How come when men cook outdoors it's 'barbecuing',
but when women do it it's 'witchcraft'?"

"Peter Pan, the Utensil that Never Grew Up"

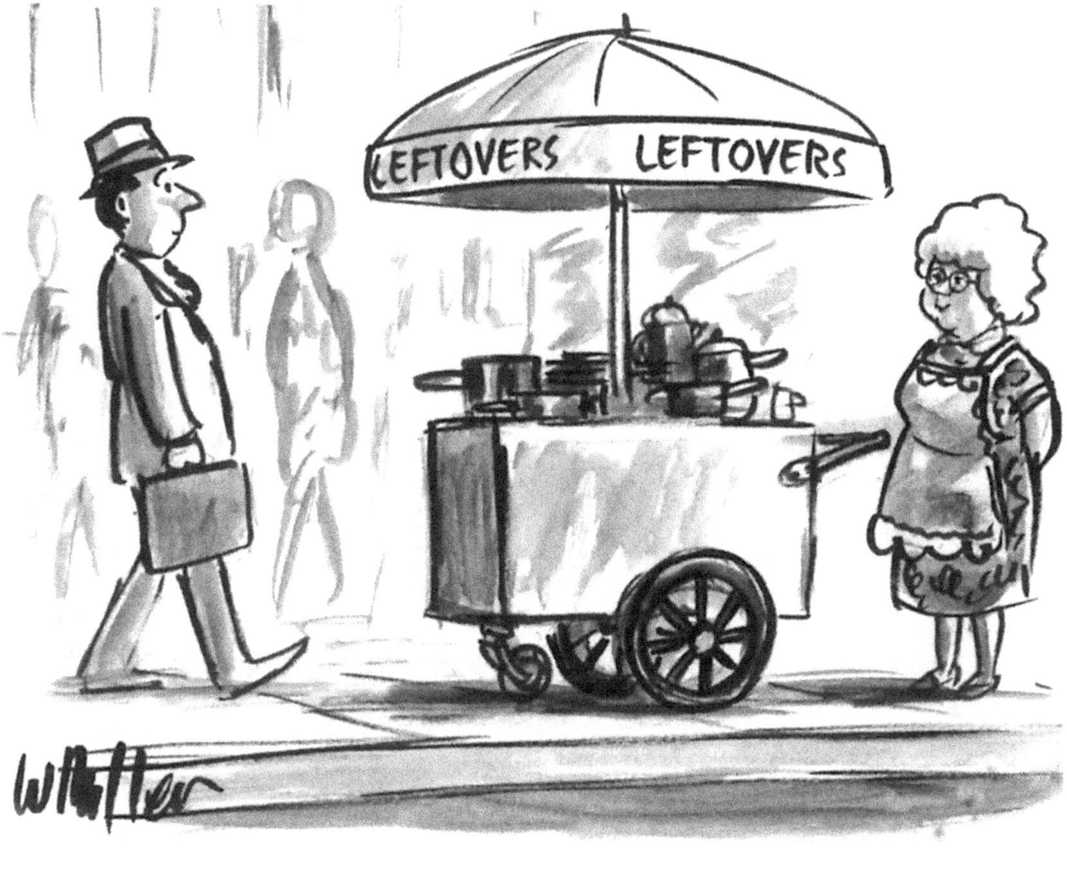
LEFTOVERS LEFTOVERS

"Whoa! That's a lot of flame, Beth. I'll pick up a
fire extinguisher on my way back from the gym."

MOM & DAD RECIPE CORNER

Super-Duper Meat Loaf

Prepare meat loaf as usual, but add one cup of minced broccoli. Serve with a secret smile.

Heh, heh.

Yummy Tacos

Use one of those kits, but sneak in one cup of minced cauliflower. Act all innocent while serving.

Who, me?

Awesome Franks 'n' Beans

Franks, beans, and a cup of minced spinach that somehow "got in there."

Doesn't that beat all!

World's Best Chocolate Cake

If anyone acts suspicious, or starts asking questions, you know **nothing**.

"Cabbage in chocolate cake"?

That's ABSURD!

r. Chst

"The bagels—they just keep getting bigger, no?"

"You're in for a treat—Gregor awoke this morning from uneasy dreams to find himself transformed into a killer tapas chef."

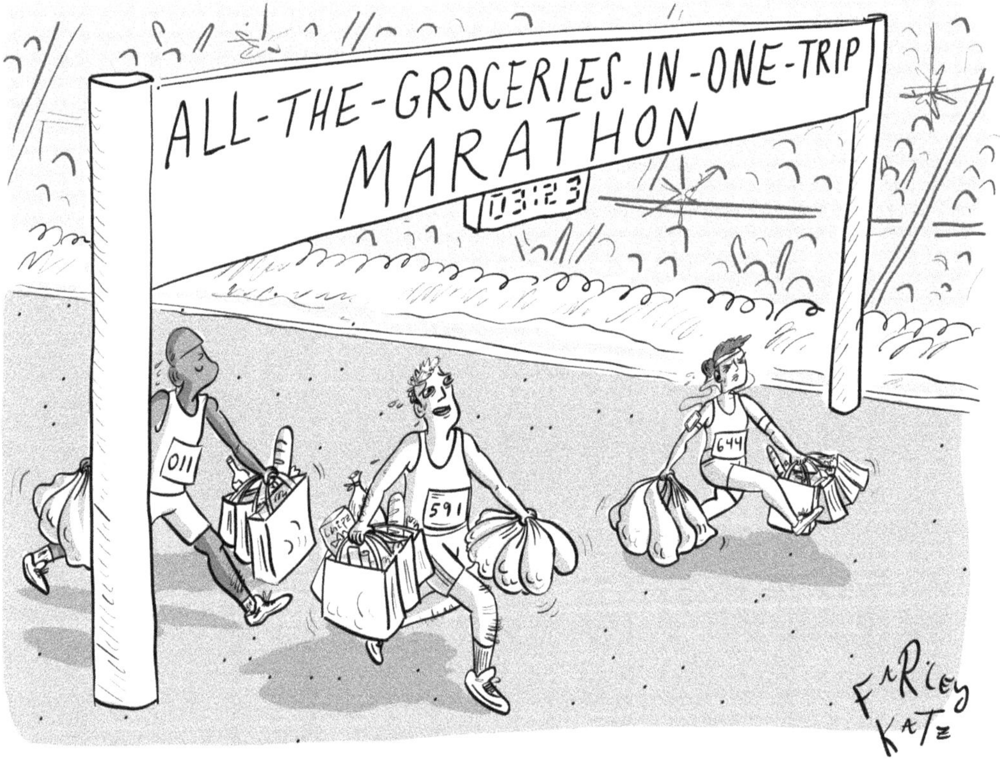
ALL-THE-GROCERIES-IN-ONE-TRIP
MARATHON
03:23
011
591
644
FARLEY KATZ

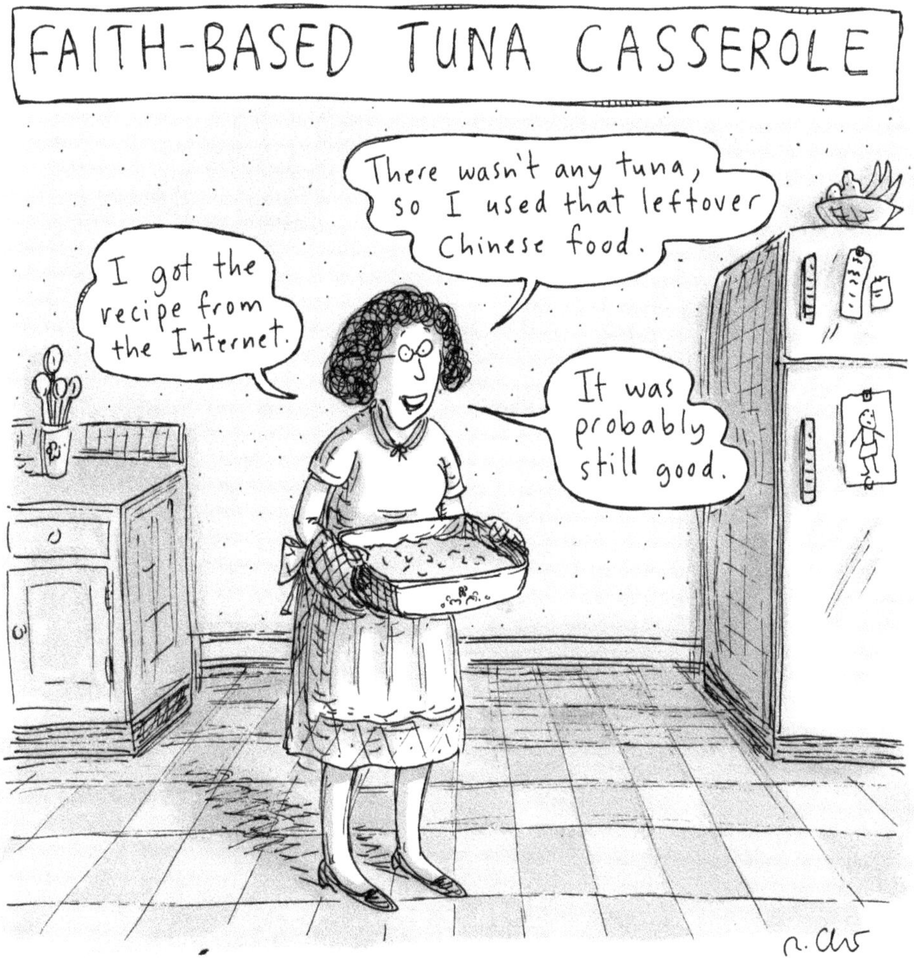

FAITH-BASED TUNA CASSEROLE
I got the recipe from the Internet.
There wasn't any tuna, so I used that leftover Chinese food.
It was probably still good.

THE TRUE STORY OF

VANILLA PUDDING

Who invented it? Why, Mrs Mary Evans, of course!

Did you buy anything?

Let me see... No, I did not

And what were the circumstances, exactly?

I think it was a Tuesday

By the way, where does Mrs Golgarsh come into this?

That woman is the biggest recipe thief for miles around. She does not come into this at all.

And then what happened?

The doorbell rang. Somebody was selling something

Why do you call it "vanilla pudding"?

Well, when I tasted it, it tasted just like vanilla pudding. Hence its name.

r. Chast

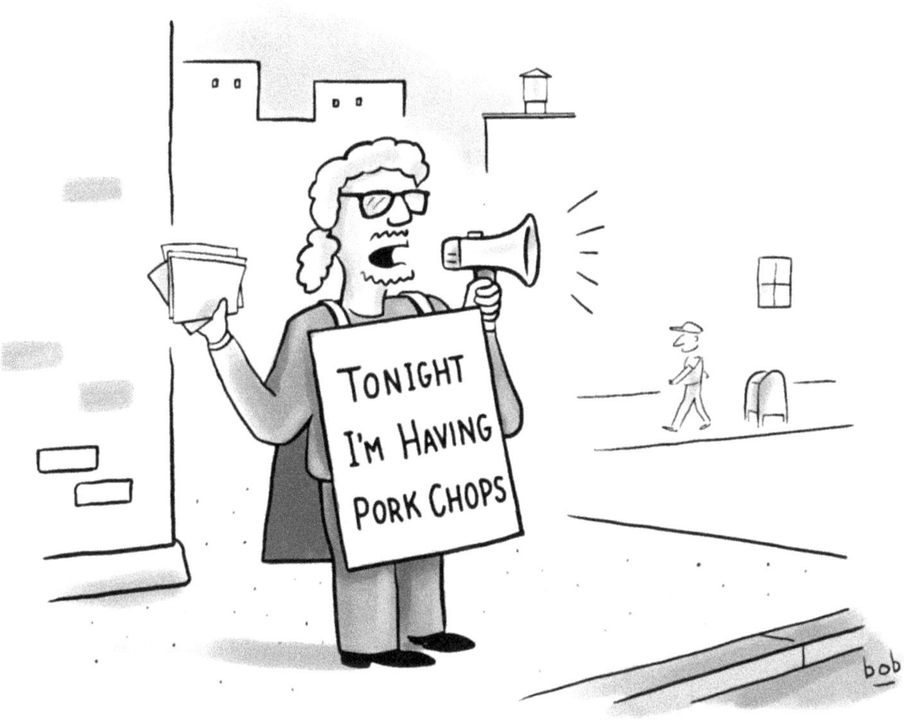
TONIGHT I'M HAVING PORK CHOPS
bob

BEFORE FACEBOOK

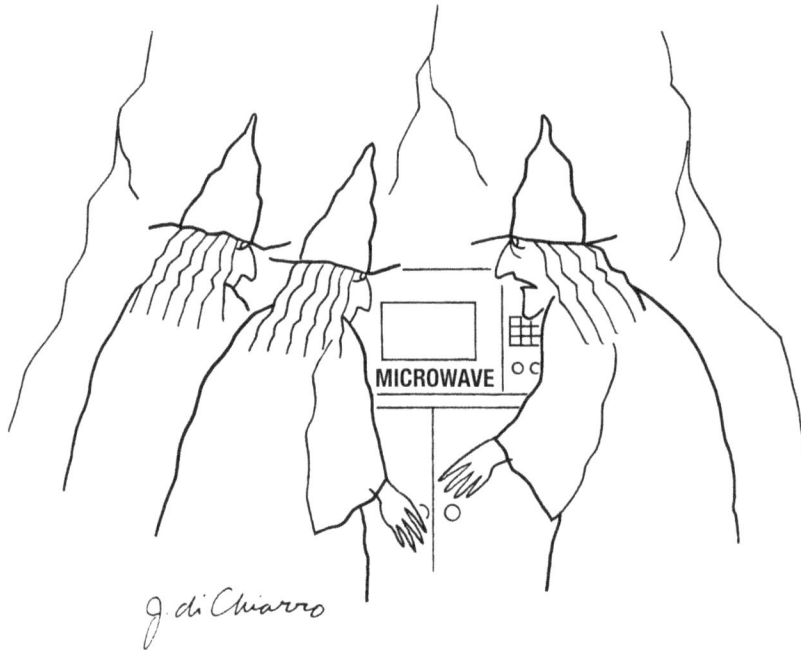

"I miss the 'boil and bubble', but it saves a lot of time."

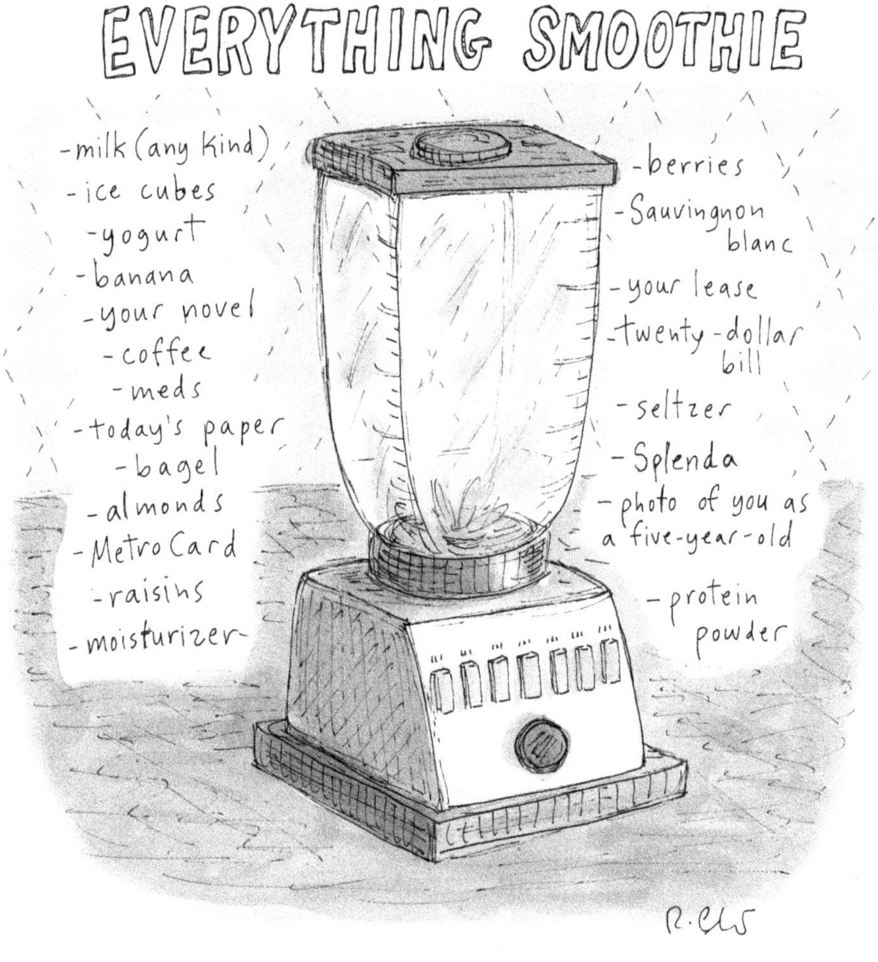
EVERYTHING SMOOTHIE
-milk (any kind)
-ice cubes
-yogurt
-banana
-your novel
-coffee
-meds
-today's paper
-bagel
-almonds
-MetroCard
-raisins
-moisturizer
-berries
-Sauvingnon blanc
-your lease
-twenty-dollar bill
-seltzer
-Splenda
-photo of you as a five-year-old
-protein powder

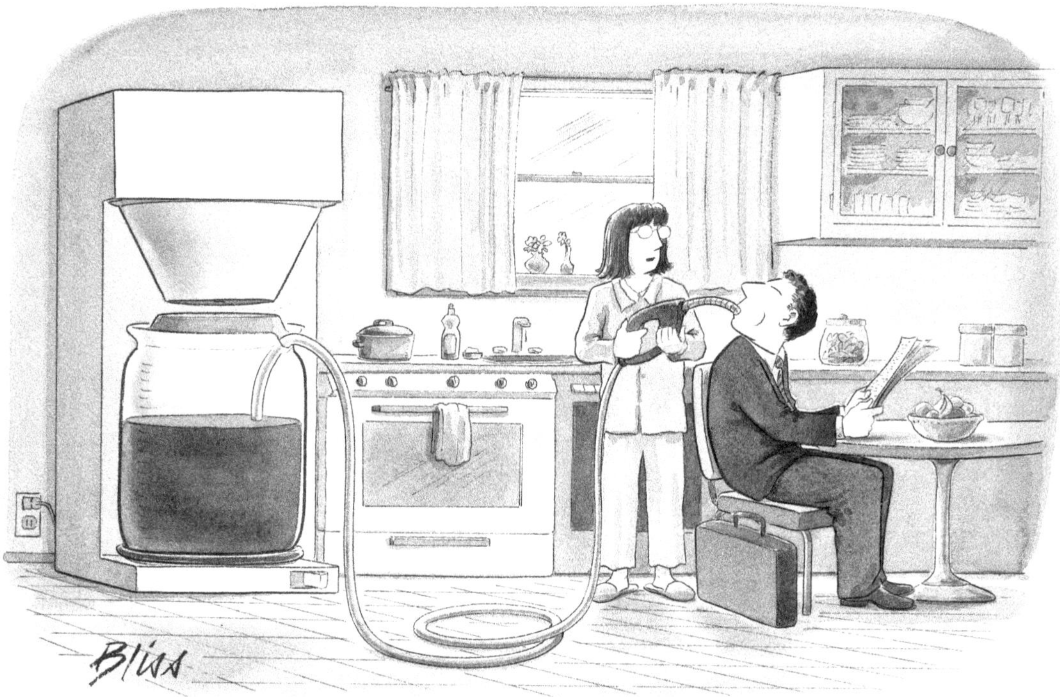

BLISS

"Say when."

"It's so nice to gather and enjoy
a simple home-cooked meal together."

Index of Artists

www.ingramcontent.com/pod-product-compliance
Lightning Source LLC
Chambersburg PA
CBHW040847100426
42813CB00015B/2738